THE ART OF POETRY OF HORACE;

THE ART OF POETRY OF HORACE;

Horace and Daniel Bagot

www.General-Books.net

Publication Data:

Title: The Art of Poetry of Horace
Author: Horace and Daniel Bagot
General Books publication date: 2009
Original publication date: 1880
Original Publisher: William Blackwood and Sons
Subjects: Law / General
Law / Administrative Law Regulatory Practice
Law / Civil Procedure
Law / Constitutional
Law / International
Poetry / General
Poetry / American / General

1

SECTION 1

ARS POETICA.

Humano capiti cervicem pictor equinam
Jungcrc si velit, et varias induccre plumaa
Uncli(iuo collatis membris, ut turpitcr atnnn
Dcsiuat in pisccni muliur formosa supcnic;
Spcctatum admissi risum tenealis, amici ? 5
Credite, Pisones, isti tabulse fore librum
Fcrsimilem, cujus, vclut sugri somnia, vanse
Fingentur species, xit nee pes nee cnput uni
Beddatur formse. Pictoribus atque poetis

Ip a painter should take a fancy to join a horse's neck to a human head, and to spread the plumage of variously coloured l)irds over limbs collected from animals of every country, so that a comely woman above should disgustingly terminate in a horrible-looking fish; if admitted to see the sight, could you, my friends, refrain from laughter ? Believe me, Pisos, that n book would be very similar to a painting like that, of which the constituent ideas shall be formed so fanciful and absurd, like a sick man's dreams, as that neither foot nor head, *neitlier end nor beginning,* can be reduced to an agreement with one uniform and consistent model. To painters and to poets, *you* TIIE ART OF POETRY.

Suppose a painter, by his fancy led,
Should join a horse's neck and human head,
And upon limbs from various beasts should bring
Plumage from birds of every coloured wing,
So that a handsome female face should grow
Down to a fish of hideous form below,
Could you, this picture if allowed to see,
Gaze 011 the sight and keep from laughter free *1*
Believe me, Pisos, such a sketch as this
Supplies an emblem for a book that is 10
Filled with absurd fantastic thoughts that seem
Like the chimeras of a sick man's dream,
So that a reader cannot judge or scan
A work like this as one consistent plan.
4 *A Poem should have*
Quidlibet muletuli semper fuit ajqua potestas. 10
Scimus, et hanc veniam petimusque damusque vicissim;
Sed non ut placidis coeant immitia; non ut
Serpentes avibus geminentur, tigribus agni.
Inceptis gravibus plerumque et magna professis, rururqus late qui splcndcat, umia ct alter 15
Assuitur paunus ; cum lucus et ara Dianro,
Kt properantis aquaj per amrcnos ambitus agros,
Aut llumcn Ilhcnum, aut pluvius describitur arcus.
Sed nunc nou erat his locus. Et fortasse cupressum
Scis simulare: quid hoc, si fractis enatat exspes 20
Navibus, sere dato qui pingitur ? amphora cccpit
Institui; currente rota, cur urceus exit ?

will say, there has always liecn conceded an equal privilege of adventuring anything bold and daring. We are aware of this, and wo both seek for this indulgence for ourselves *when we write,* and grant it to others in their turn *when we act at critics,* but not to the extent that what arc savage should coalesce with what arc mild, not to the extent that serpents should be coupled with birds, *or* lambs with tigers.

It often happens that to grave and pompons commencements, and such as inaku great and ostentatious professions, one or two shreds of purple patchwork, *at it were,* that may give a diffusive brilliancy *to the ityle,* are stitched on :'as when the grove and altar of Diann, and meandering streams of water swiftly flowing through a delightful country, or the river Hhinc, or the rainbow, arc deHcrihcd. Itut in the coau which I am supposing tlieru i no room for these *mere- IricioHt cntlii'llisliiiu-uti.* Perhaps, too, you can sketch a cyprtm Of what use is tins skill of yours, if he who is being painted by you for payment, is swimming hopeless from a shipwreck ;' You begin to form a largo vase ; as the wheel revolves, why does a small pitcher conu- forth ? In short, write or make what you will,

Unity and Consistency. 5
You'll say that painters, and that poets too,
Have power whate'er they wish to dare and do ;
We freely grant it, and the right we claim,
Prepared for others to concede the same,
But not to join what's fierce with what is mild,
That lambs with tigers should be reconciled. 20

To grand exordiums, and which promise much, There's often tacked some purple patchwork, such As when Diana's grove and altar shine In glowing terms in some ambitious line: And winding streams through pleasing landscapes flow, Or the grand Rhine, or heaven's sun-tinted bow. But all such tinsels here are out of place, They mar the poem, and its style deface. Perhaps you know a cypress how to paint, While ho who hires your skill is weak and faint, 30 . Struggling to leave the wreck and reach the shore, He wants a votive tablet and no more. A vase is planned, but as the wheel you turn, Why, then, comes forth a poor and jMdtry urn ?

6 *The Cause of*
Denique sit quidvis, simplex duntaxat et unum.

Maxima pars vatum, pater et juvenes patre digui, Decipimur specie recti. Brevis esse laboro, 25

Obscurus fio; sectantem lenia nervi
Deficiunt animique; professus grandia turget;
Serpit Immi tutus uimium timidusque proccllui.
Qui variaro cupit rom prodigialiter unam,
Delphiuum silvis appingit, fluctibus aprum. 30
In vitium ducit culpse fuga, si caret arte.

let it only be characterised by a simplicity and unity of design throughout.

A large majority of us poets – I address you the father, and you young men worthy of having such a father – are deceived by a semblance of what is right, *or by the estimate which we form for ourselves of wlutt we think should constitute the correctness and beauty of poetic composition.* For example, I endeavour to be concise and sententious, I become obscure and unintelligible. Nerve and spirit fail him who aims at a refined and easy style. Hc who aspires to the sublime and majestic, becomes turgid and bombastical. Ho who is too cautious and apprehensive of a storm, creeps along the ground; *or, in other words, he who is sensitively and over scrupulously afraid uf a too soaring and lofty style, degenerates into what is Imo and gruvelliny.* He who is anxious to diversify and impart variety to a simple subject, by ingrafting upon it marvellous and sensational incidents, paints a dolphin in the woods, or a boar amongst the waves. , The very attempt to avoid a fault leads to a vicious error, if there be a deficiency of judicious and well-discipliuud tact.

28. This iine might aiso be rendered thus : –

" Like to the man who creeps aiong the shore, And droaUn to hoist a saii or iiit nil oar."

Faults in Style. 7
A work of art should have a single aim,
And be throughout from first to last the same.

Most of us poets oft are led astray
By what wo thiiik to be the better way.
Concise and brief in style I strive to be,
I find I'm landed in obscurity: 40
I seek a smooth and polished style to reach,
A want of nerve effeminates my speech :
He that aspires to grand and lofty themes,
Becomes inflated and bombastic seems :
He that too timorous quivers at a storm,
Shrinks as a victim to a false alarm,
And, like the bird that dreads a wintry sky,
Creeps- on the ground, afraid to soaj or fly.
He that desires with wonders to enrich
A simple theme that wants no startling speech, 50
Goes to the length of painting out of place,
Boars amidst waves, and dolphins in the grass.
While we a blemish with much caution shun,
Into a fault from want of skill we run.

On the Choice of

Emilium circa ludum faber imus et ungues Exprimet, et molles imitabitur sere capillos; Infeb!x operis Bumma, quia ponere totum Nesciet. Hunc ego me, si quid componere curcm, 35 Non magis ease velim, quam naso vivere pravo, Spectandum nigris oculis nigroque capillo.

Sumite materiam vestris, qui scribitis, sequam Viribus; et versate diu, quid ferre recusent, Quid valeant humeri. Cui lecta potenter erit res, 40 Nee facimdia deseret hunc nec lucidus ordo.

Ordinis hsec virtus erit et Venus, aut ego fallor,

A sculptor of the lowest class near the /luniliuu school will represent nails and imitate delicate hair in brass, while ho is unfortunate in the grand outline of his work, because he is deficient in skill to model the entire figure. I would no more wish to be such an artist as this, if I were anxious to compose anything, than to be a living man with a disfigured nose, though remarkable for having black eyes and black hair.

I advise you who are going to write to choose a subject commensurate with your capacity, and consider for a long time what your mental powers refuse, and what they are able to sustain. Neither eloquent fluency of language nor perspicuity of arrangement will be wanting to that man whose theme shall have been selected in proportion to his ability, *or with a view to what lie is able to execute.*

This, or I arn mistaken, will constitute the excellence and elegance of proper systematic arrangement,

a Suitable Subject. 9

A tenth-rate workman near the Emilian school
Will model nails correctly and by rule,
Will in the brass soft flowing tresses mould,
Tresses that look like burnished threads of gold,
Unlucky yet, from want of art or plan,

To finish off a perfect form of man. 60
If I should care a poem to compose,
I would not be an artist such as those,
As I'd not like with ugly nose to appear,
Though famed for jet-black eyes and raven hair.
Choose, you that write, a subject of a kind
That suits the strength and stature of your miud;
And ponder long, and scrutinise with care,
What they refuse and what they've nerve to bear.
He that selects with this sound rule in view,
Will write with freedom and with clearness too, 70
In words that shall with eloquence express
His thoughts in asy flow and lucid dress.
In this the merit, for I know it well, And beauty of arrangement mainly dwell,10

The Arrangement of the Parts

Ut jam nunc dicat jam nunc debentia dici,
Pleraque differat et pnesens in tempus omittat,
Hoc amet, hoc spernat, promissi carminis auctor. 45
In verbis etiam tenuis cautusque serendis,
Dixeris egregie, uotum si callida verbum
Beddiderit junctura novum. Si forte necesse est
Indiciis monstrare recentibus abdita rerum,
Fingere cinctutis non exaudita Ccthegis 50
Continget; dabiturque licentia sumpta pudenter.
Et nova fictaque nuper habebunt verba fidem, si
Grseco fonte cadent, parce detorta. Quid autem

that the author of a promised and projected poem *thould be careful a to theprvper time for introducing the incidents of his subject, 10 tint! he* should say at uach particular time what should bo said at that particular time, that he should, *wlurever necessary,* keep in reserve and omit a good deal for the present, that he should *exercise discrimination in resolving to* adopt one topic and to reject another.

Using also a judicious and discerning carefulness in the selection and disposition of wonts, you will have expressed yourself with peculiar elegance if an ingenious association shall have impressed upon a familiar word an aspect of freshness and novelty. If yon / should, perhaps, have occasion to explain some abstruse, or hitherto unknown subjects, by new symbols or modes of representation, you will have to invent terms which were never heard of by our old-fushioncd ancestors; and such a licence, if used with moderation, will bo freely conceded to you. And wonts which are new and lately coined will havu credit and currency, if they flow from a Grecian source with a Very slight deviation. But why will the Roman grant to Cmcilius and Plautus a privi-

and the Choice of Words. 11
That he who writes a book we hope to see,
Should range his matter in its due degree,
That every thought should shine with well-timed grace,

And each detail should fill its proper place, [choose,
Some thoughts postpone, and some with care should
Some as unworthy of his verse refuse. 80
The choice of words must be attended to,
Nice combinations make an old one new.
A word that's known a novel sense will find
With a fresh theme by dexterous art combined.
If you require to speak of things abstruse,
Or to describe what's only just in use,
You may invent expressions of your own,
Such as to ancient Romans were unknown :
But if you would this privilege preserve,
You must employ it with discreet reserve. 90
Words new and lately made will credit know
If, slightly turned, from Grecian fonts they flow.
But why should Roman critics take from one
A right that critics should refuse to none ?
12 *The Inventing of New Words*
Csecilio Plautoque dabit Romanus ademptum
Virgilio Varioque ? Ego cur, acquirers pauca 55
Si possum, invideor, cum lingua Catonis et Enni
Sermonem patrium ditaverit, et nova rerum
Nomina protulerit ? Licuit semperque licebit
Signature pnesente nota producere nomen.
Ut silviD foliis pronos mutantur in annos; 60
Prima cadunt: ita verborum vetus interit ictas,
Et juvenum ritu florent modo nata vigentque.
Debemur morti nos nostraque: sive receptus
Terra Neptunus classes Aquilonibus arcet,
lege which is refused to Virgil and Varius ? Why am I invidiously carped at, if I can make the acquisition of a fuw words, when the diction of Cato and Enmus has enriched the vocabulary of their native land, and has produced new names for objects ? It has ever been allowable, and always will be, to bring forward into use a word which bean the impression of the current stamp, or ir/u7t u *formed in compliance with On idiom prevailing at tlie time.* As woods are changed with respect to their leaves as years decline – those of earliest growth are tho first that full – Ho thu old generation of words dies off, and those which are of recent production display a freshness and vigour like young men. We and our works are doomed and destined to dissolution. Whether Neptune received into the land *so as to form a harbour of refuge* defends our fleets from north winds – the enterprise of a king ; and the lake, for a long time unproductive and fit to be navi-
and the Decay of Old. 13
Csecilius, Plautus, first put in their claim,
Virgil and Varius may assert the same.
If I, for instance, can command a few

Words of a novel form nnd fashion new,
Why should the tooth of envy press on me,
When Cato and when Ennius are free . 100
To enrich their native tongue with words that hold
A sterling worth, like coins of sterling gold ?
Poetic licence always must allow,
As in time past, to modem authors now,
Leave to present for public use and view
Words that like coins arc stamped with impress -new.
As leaves are changed while gliding years go round,
Those that bloom first, first strew the forest ground,
So words grow old and in their course must die,
While fresh and youthful words their place supply.
We and our own productions must decay, 111
Death's ebbing tide shall sweep them all away.
That kingly work, where Neptune leaves the sea,
Enters the land by Csesar's wise decree,
14 *Words die like all*
Regis opus ; sterilisque diu palus, aptaque remis, 65
Vicinas urbes alit et grave sentit aratrum ;
Seu cursum mutavit iniquum frugibus amnis,
Doctus iter melius: mortalia facta peribunt,
Nedum sermonum stet honos et gratia vivax.
Multa renascentur quro jam cecidere, cadentque 70
Quse nunc sunt in honore vocabula, si volet usus,
Quem penes arbitrium est et jus et nonna loquendi.
Res gestse regumque ducumque et tristia bella
Quo scribi possent numero, monstravit Homerus.
Versibus iinpariter junctis querimonia primum, 75
Post etiam inclnsa est voti sontentia compos

,-iiteil by rowing vends, now Ri1pports neighbouring towns and feels the ponderous plough; or the river, taught to run in a better direction, has changed its former course, which was injurious to the crops : *these* achievements of mortal men must perish; much less can the credit and popularity of words and phrases be of long duration. Many shall spring up again which have now become obsolete, and those which are now in fashion and repute shall fall into disuse, if common custom shall decree it, in which is vested the power of arbitrarily deciding, the right of legislating, and the privilege of determining, what shall be the recognised rule and standard of language.

Homer has shown in what poetic measure – *namely, in the epic* – the exploits of kings and military commanders, and disastrous wars may be described.

Plaintive subjects, or dirges, were first treated in unequal elegiac numbers, *consisting of alternate hexameters and pentameters;* afterwards themes which described the feelings and sensations of lovers succeeding in their desires, *or the conquests of love,* were included in this kind of verse. But as to the author who first intnxlucc'd elegiac measures, which are short

the Works of Man. 15
Aud forms a refuge from the northern wind,
Where fleets may float in waters calm and kind;
The marsh, once barren and unfruitful, now
Feeds neighbouring towns and feels the crushing plough;
The Tiber turns, obedient to command,
Its course injurious to the fertile land : 120
Those works must perish, man's achievements die,
Much less can words the will of fate defy.
Words are but flowers, the blossoms of a day,
Their bloom must vanish, and their grace decay :
Many shall rise and spring to life again,
And like as withered brandies strew thc plain,
Many shall fall and out of fashion go,
Their credit lost, if use will have it so –
Use that enacts with 'arbitrary sway
The laws of speech which authors must obey. 130
Sad wars of chicfs, and grand exploits of kings,
In epic verse immortal Homer sings.
First plaintive strains lines elegiac move,
Then vows of lovers realised in love ;
16 *The Different Kinds of Poetry*
Quis tamen exiguos elegos emiserit auctor,
Grammatici certant, et adhuc sub judice l!s cst.
Archilochum proprio rabies armavit iambo:
Hunc socci cepere pedem, grandesque cothurni, 80
Alternis aptum sermonibus, et populares
Vincentem strepitus, et natum rebus agendis.

Musa dedit fidibus divos, puerosque deorum, Et pugilem victorem, ot equum certamine primum, Et juvenum curas, et libera vina referre. 85

Descriptas servare vices operumque colores, Cur ego, si nequeo ignoroque, poeta salutor ?

and humble as *compared with the epic,* philologists have a controversy, and the case is still before the judge, *awl remains undecided.*

Ilis raging spirit armed Archilochus with the iambic, which was peculiarly his own. Then socks and stateiy buskins adopted this measure *for comic and trayic compositions,* as suitable for conversational scenes, and calculated to drown the noise of the people, and adapted for occasions when incidents in the drama were to be visibly enacted on the stage.

The muse bas assigned to the lyre the olBce of celebrating gods, and the sons of gods, and the victorious pugilist, and the home foremost in the nice, and the anxious courtships of young people, and the loose and unrestrained revelries of wine.

If I have neither the natural ability nor the acquired skill to observe the distinct departments of each kind of poetry, as they, have been described, und the various shades and complexions of poetic production, why am 1 styled and saluted as a poet ? why

and tlie Metre Proper for each. 17
But who first planned the elegiac line,
Grammarians argue, critics can't divine.
The Parian poet first iambics used,
Through these his raging passion was diffused;
Then socks and buskins next assumed this kind,
For comic scenes and tragic acts designed, 140
Suited a part in dialogues to take,
And noisy crowds a listening audience make ;
And when we witness actions on the stage,
Iambic measures best our ears engage.
Of gods, and sons of gods, victoribus men,
The steed that conquers on Olympia's plain,
The pleasing pains that love's young dreams impart,
And the free joys of wine that cheers the heart,
To sing such themes with mild poetic fire
The muse has granted to the soothing lyre. 150
If I these nice distinctions cannot mtnd,
For every work its right complexion find,
Why should I seek with empty pride to claim
A poet's talents or a poet's fame ?
18 *The Distinctive Style of*
Cur nescire, pudens prave, quam discere molo ?
Versibus exponi tragicis res comica non vult: Indignatnr item privatis ac prope socco 90
DignU carminibus narrari coena Thyestse.
Singula quseque locum teneant sortita decenter.
Interdum tamen et vocem comcedia tollit,
Iratusque Chremes tnmido delitigat ore;
Et tragicus plerumque dolet sermone pedestri. 95.
Telephus et Peleus, cum pauper et exul uterque,
Projicit ampullae et sesquipedalia verba,
Si curat cor spectantis tetigisse querela.
Non satis est pulchra esse poemata; dulcia sun to, Et quocunque volent animum auditoris agunto. 100
do I prefer, through a culpable affectation of modesty, to remain ignorant rather than to learn ?

A comic theme does not like to be ostentatiously represented in tragic verses. And on the same principle such a subject as the banquet of Thyestes disdains to be described in verses that are common and familiar, and almost fit for comedy. Let each kind of poetic composition maintain with propriety the peculiar place to which it legitimately belongs. Yet sometimes even comedy raises her voice *and adoptt a more stately and elevated tone,* and the irritated Chremes foams and rages in a blustering and swelling strain ; and a tragic character generally gives expression to grief in a humble and prosaic style. Telephus and Peleus, *for example,* when both are in poverty and in exile, throw aside great swelling phrases and hyper-elongated words, if they care to make an impression upon the heart of the spectator by their complaints.

It is not enough that poems be showy and beautiful; they should also be affecting and interesting, and should carry away the mind of the auditor wherever they wish, *exercising an absolute*

Comic and Tragic Poems. 19
Why not prefer such knowledge to acquire,
Than, falsely modest, uninformed retire ?
A comic subject does not wish to be
Displayed in verses fit for tragedy:
Thus, too, Thyestes' banquet would disdain
Language familiar and of comic strain. 160
Let each description hold its proper place,
And act its part with seemliness and grace.
Yet sometimes comedy will raise her style,
And Chremes with inflated words revile ;
And tragic actors mostly wish to reach,
When griefs expressed, an humble form of speech.
Kings, poor and exiled, must this law respect,
And words magniloquent in sound reject;
Must shun bombastic talk with due restraint,
If they would move us with their sad complaint. 170
Tis not enough that'poems should be fine,
A pleasing air should breathe through'every line :
They should have power with easy chain to bear
Where'er they wish the minds of those who hear.
20 *The Language should correspond*
Ut ridentibus arrident, ita flentibus adsunt
Human! vultus. Si vis me Here, dolendum est
Primum ipsi tibi; time tua me infortunia lsedent,
Telephe vel Peleu. Male si mandata loqueris,
Aut dormitabo aut ridebo. Tristia moestum 105
Vultum verba decent; iratum plena minarum;
Ludentem lasciva; severum seria dictu.
Format enim natura prius nos intus ad omnem
Fortunarum habitum; juvat, aut impellit ad iram,
command over his passions and feelings. As human features put on a smile with those who smile, so do they sympathise with those who weep.'. IT you wish mo to Bhed tears of compassion, you must first manifest grief yourself; then, Telephut) anil FulcuB, your calamities will affuct me with a painful interest. If you give expression to what is committed to you, in an unsuitable tone or manner, I shall either go to sleep or I shall laugh. Sorrowful and pathetic words suit a sad and dejected countenance; words of a menacing tone suit on angry one ; words of a gay tone suit a playful one;

serious words suit a countenance of a grave and severe aspect. For nature, in tho first instance, moulds the original constitution of our moral being so that our inward feelings can be adapted to every modification of external fortune : she produces in us the sensation of delight,

with tfie Inward Feelings, 21
Just as the human face will smiles return
To those who smile, it mourns with those who mourn.
If you desire that I should weep, you must
In your own sorrow moke me put my trust:
First grieve yourself, then your misfortunes will A
My soul with sympathy and sadness fill. 180
If you your parts unfittingly recite,
I'll cither doze away or laugh outright.
Sad words become a countenance that's sad,
Words that breathe threatenings those with anger mad :
He that is playful speaks in sportive strains, ,
He that's austere in serious words complains;
For nature shapes the moral frame of man
On this instinctive sympathetic plan, –
Whatever form external fortune takes,
She by a force of inward impulse makes . 190
Our hearts to have impressions that agree
With what we feel, and what we hear, and sec:
Now she inspires us with ecstatic joys,
In anger next our passions she employs,
22 and with the Ages and
Aut ad humum moerore gravi deducit et angit; no
Post effert animi motus interprete lingua.
Si dicentis erunt fortunis absona dicta,
Komani tollent equites peditesque cachinnum.
Intererit multum divusne loquatur, an heros,
Maturusne senex, an adhuc florente juventa 115
Fervidus; an matrona potens, an sedula nutrix ;
Mercatorne vagus, cultorne virentis agelli;
Colchus an Assyrius; Thebis nutritus an Argis.

Aut famafn sequere, aut sibi convenientia finge, Scriptor. Honoratum si forte reponis Achillem ; 120 Impiger, iracundus, inexorabilis, acer,

or impels us to anger, or sinks mid depresses to tho very grou'ml, and racks Uh with overwhelming grief, then slia brings out thusu emotions of the mind *into vocal expression* by the tongue as the *soul's* interpreter. If what is spoken shall not harmonise with the rank and circumstances of the speaker, Roman knighta and plebeians will strike up a violent laugh. It will make a material difference whether a god is speaking, or a hero, or an old man of ripe experience and mature knowledge of the world, or a young man still glowing with the bloom of youth ; or a domineering and consequential old lady, or a busy and officious nurse; a travelling merchant, or the cultivator of a flourishing farm ; a Colchian or an Assyrian; a person educated at Thebes, or at Argos.

Either follow historical tradition when you write, or, if you invent, construct incidents and characters which will bo consistent with themselves. If, perhaps, you reproduce a representation of the ennobled Achilles, let him be described as energetic and intrepid in action, wrathful, implacable, and impetuous ; let him

Circumstances of the Characters. 23

Or to the ground with crushing grief she brings,
With heaving pain our anguished souls she wrings;
Then, when she forms these motions in the mind,
By language next to others they're defined.
If what is said won't suit the speaker's state,
A peal of laughter's heard from every seat: 200
Plebeian Romans and the Roman knight
Know well what is, by rules of acting, right.
'Twill differ much if gods upon the stage,
Or a brave hero, shall our thoughts engage ;
Whether a man maturely wise from years,
Or one that glows with blooming youth appears;
A haughty matron, or a bustling maid;
A merchant, or a man who wields a spade;
One from 'mongst Colchians or Assyrians brought,
Or one at Thebes or Argos bred and taught. 210
You'll copy fame, or if to invent you choose,
i Then what is seemly and consistent use.
Renowned Achilles you must picture well –
Wild as the storm, and hot as flames from hell;

24 *Old Characters should be described*

Jura neget sibi nata, nihil non arroget armis.
Sit Medea ferox invictaque, flebilis Ino,
Perfidus Ixion, lo vaga, tristis Orestes.
Si quid inexpertum scense committis, et audes 125
Personam formare novam, servetur ad imum
Qualis ab incepto processerit et sibi constet.
Difficile est proprie communia dicere, tuque
Rectius Iliacum carmen deducis iu actus,
Quam si proferres ignota indictaque primus. 130

deny that laws were ever made for him, let him indignantly insist upon everything being left to the arbitration of arms. Let Medea be ferocious and relentless, Ino in tears, Ixion perfidious, lo a vagrant, Orestus sad.

' If you commit to the stage anything as yet untried, and have the confidence to form an original character *for representation,* let it be preserved to the end the some as it set out from the beginning, and let it be consistent with itself. It is difficult to treat subjects as yet unappropriated, and which all have therefore a common right to select, in such a peculiar style as to individualise them, or to make them your own ;

and, in fact, you will find it more easy to comply with the rules of dramatic com- 1
position by reducing the ' Iliad' into acts, than if you are the I first to bring forward
themes which are unknown, and which I, have not been treated by any former poet.
A subject which has

agreeable to their History. 25
Impetuous passion surging in hie mind,
No prayers can move him, and no laws can bind;
Swords are his umpires, and his rule of right
The blazing battle and the scorching fight.
Lot fierce Medea tread the tragic stage,
Impersonation of unconquered rage, 220
Ino in tears, Ixiou false and bad,
Io a vagrant, and Orestes sad.
Should you a scene as yet untried produce,
And a new style of person introduce,
Ho who would thus attentive listeners claim
Should be throughout consistent and the same.
Subjects as yet unused and open still,
Tis hard to manage with peculiar skill.
You'll find you will be more successful far
To choose the poem of the Trojan war, 230
And draw from it your several scenes and acts,
Than if you're first to take dramatic facts
And new inventions from an untouched store,
Unheard, unspoken, and unknown before.
26 *On Constructing a New Drama*
Publica- materies privati juris erit, si
Non circa vilem patulumque moraberis orbem ;
Nee verbum verbo curabis reddere fidus
Interprea ; nee desilies imitator in arctum,
Unde pedem proferre pudor vetet, aut operis lex. 135
Nee sic incipies ut scriptor cyclicus olim :
" Fortunam Priami cantabo et nobilo bellum."
Quid dignum tanto feret hie promissor hiatu ?
Parturiunt montes, nascetur ridiculus mus.
Quanto rectius hie qui nil molitur inepte – 140

become public by having been already treated, *tudi at the ' Iliad,'* will justly become
your private and personal property if you will not waste your time in dilating on a
common und obvious round *if trite and trivial incidents,* nor, as a too scrupulously
exact interpreter, be over careful to render word for word, nor as an imitator start away
into a position in which you are cramped 61; *resolving on a too minutely-defined plan,
in which you propose to bring forward all the facts and details of the original story,*
from which position either your diffidence as an author, or the law which regulates
the execution of your adopted style of composition, will prevent you from retreating.
Nor should you begin in the way that a strolling ballad-monger once did – " I shall

sing of the destiny of Priam and the famous Trojan war." What will this braggadocio say worthy of such blustering bombast ? Mountains are in labour: a ridiculous mouse will be born. How much more in compliance with the art of poetry docs he begin who attempts nothing injudiciously or unskilfully! "Tell me,

from old Materials. 27
What has been used you'll make by right your
own,
If you don't waste your time on things well known ;
Nor care to be so slavishly absurd
As to translate your author word for word ;
Nor when you imitate his grand design,
Detail again what's told in every line, 240
Thus cramp yourself within a narrow span,
Whence neither shame nor rules of writing can ,
Let you escape to be at ease and free
To think and write, as poets ought to be.
Nor thus begin as once a scribbler wrote –
"king Priam's Fate And That Grand War Of
NOTE
I'll Sing." What can this vaunting boaster tell ?
His promise sounds so like an auction-bell.
Mountains are seized with labour's pangs and fears,
Laughter is caused when one small mouse appears. 250
How much superior is the easy way
Of him whose genius never goes astray –
28 . *The Excellencies of Homer*
" Die mihi, Musa, virum, captse post tempora Trojse,
Qui mores hominum multorum vidit et urbes."
Non fumum ex fulgore, sed ex fumo dare lucem
Cogitat, ut speciosa dehinc miracula promat, 144
Antiphaten, Scyllamque, et cum Cy elope Charybdin.
Nee reditum Diomedis ab interitu Meleagri,
Nee gemino bellum Trojanum orditur ab ovo.
Semper ad eventum festinat, et in medias res,
Non secus ac notas, auditorem rapit, et quse
Desperat tractata nitescere posse relinquit. 150

0 Muse 1 of the man who, after Troy was taken, inspected the manners and customs of many people, and their cities." His purpose is not to bring smoke out of a blaze, but out of smoke to produce light, that ho may then bring forward his bright and brilliant wonders, *such as* Antiphates and Scylla, and the Cyclops and Chorybdis. Nor does he begin an account of the return of Diomede from the death of Meleager, nor a history of the Trojan war from the two eggs of Leda. He always hastens on to the grand catastrophe, and hurries his reader into the very midst of the incidents of his subject, as if they were well known; and what he despairs of being capable of acquiring brilliancy from his treatment of them he at once abandons. And he so con-

supply Rules and a Model. 29
" Tell me, 0 Muse I of him who, after Troy
Was taken, did some fleeting years employ,
That laws and cities his own eyes might trace
Of men of various climes and differing race."
His aim is not to blaze, then smoke away,
But to go on from dawn to perfect day.
Thus to bring forth his wonders into view,
Scylla, Charybdis, and the Cyclops too; 260
Antiphates, *the savage king who fed
On human flesh, as he would eat up. bread.*
He goes not back to scenes that don't belong
To the main theme and purport of his song,
Nor start the tale of Diomcde's return,
From Meleager's sad funereal urn,
Nor date his story of the Trojan war
From Lcda's eggs, to trace it back so far.
He always hastens to his chief design,
Transports his reader in his foremost line 270
Into the midst of scenes as if well known,
And what he fears won't shine he lets alone.
30 *The Peculiarities of*
Atque ita mentitur, sic veris falsa remiscet,
Primo ne medium, medio ne discrepet imum.
Tu, quid ego, et populus mecum desideret, audi:
Si plausoris eges aulsea manentis, et usque
Sessuri, donee cantor " Vos plaudite " dicat; 155
JEt&tis cujusque notandi sunt tibi mores,
Mobilibuaque decor naturis dandus et annis.
Reddere qui voces jam scit pucr, ct pcde certo
Signat humum, gestit paribus colludere, et iram
Colligit ac ponit temere, et mutatur in boras. 160
Imberbis juvenis, tandem custode remote,
Invi's his fictions, so blends together what ia fabulous with what is real, that the
middle does not differ from the commencement, nor the end from the middle, *'but
there it a uniform consistency pervading the entire poem. '*
Listen to what I require, and what the people agree with me in requiring. If you
want to have an applauding spectator to wait until the curtain is drawn up, and who
will sit out the performance until the singer in the chorus shall say, " Let us have your
applause," the characteristic and distinguishing features and habits of every stage of
human life must be carefully observed, and a suitable complexion must be assigned
to the fluctuating dispositions and ages *of your characters.* The boy who now knows
how to speak, and stamps the ground with a steady and unerring footstep, delights to
play with his companions, gets into a passion, and as capriciously gets out of it, and is
changed from hour to hour. The beardless young man, whose tutor has been at length

Chttdlwod and Youlh, 31
Fictions he so expertly brings to view,
So mixes up what's feigned with what is true,
That all the parts from first to last agree
In well-sustained consistent harmony.
Now to some good advice you'll please attend:
If you would keep your audience to the end,
And hear the singer to the people say,
" We ask applause before you go away," 280
The moral features of each age of man
You must with skill and thoughtful study scan,
Assigning such complexion as appears
To suit their varying natures and their years.
The little boy who now has learned to talk,
And with sure foot along the ground to walk,
Delights with lads as young as he to play;
He's angry now, then flings his wrath away;
And like a leaf beneath the tempest's power,
He's bloion about, and changed from hour to hour.
The beardless youth, at length from tutors free, 291
Delights in noble games of chivalry;
32 *and of Manhood*
Gaudet equis canibusque et aprici gramine campi;
Cereus in vitium flecti, monitoribus asper,
Utilium tardus provisor, prodigus seris,
Sublimis, cupidusque, et anmta relinquere pernix. 165
Conversis studiis, setas animusque virilis
Quserit opes et amicitias, inservit honori,
Commisisse cavet quod mox mutare laboret.
Multa seuem circumveniunt incommoda; vel quod
Quserit, et inventis miser abstinet, ac timet uti; 170
Vel quod res omnes timide gelideque ministrat;
dismissed, takes pleasure in hones and dogs, and in the games played upon the grass of the sunny Campus Martius ; soft and pliable as wax in his tendency towards vice, sharp and rude to his advisers, slow in consulting his true interests and in providing what is really useful, extravagant of his money, aspiring and high-spirited, forming passionate attachments, and hasty in abandoning the objects of his love. His pursuits being changed, the age and intellect of his manhood are devoted to the acquisition of riches and of friendly alliances ; he is slavishly ambitious of honour and political distinction; he cautiously avoids the commission of an act which he would Boon exert himself to alter or reverse. Many discomforts surround an old man, either because he seeks to accumulate, and in a miserly spirit abstains from and is afraid to use or to enjoy what he has acquired, or because he performs everything in a hesitating and
and old Age 33
Horses and hounds his first affections gain,

Athletic sports upon the sunny plain;
Pliant as wax, to tempting vice inclined,
To those who'd give him friendly hints unkind;
Slow in providing what's of solid use ;
Of tastes expensive, thoughtlessly profuse ;
Haughty, aspiring, passionate to form
Attachments quick, yet fickle as the storm. 300
Pursuits diversified from these engage,
As years advance, his manhood mind and age;
Wealth is his idol, his ambition then
More friends, more rank, more honours to obtain ;
His reason warns him prudently to shun
A deed that soon he'd strive to have undone.
Around the man whom age and years oppress,
There's much to pain him, much to cause distress;
He seeks for wealth, and yet through fear abstains,
Like a poor miser, from his hoarded gains ; 310
In action now no longer brave and bold,
In every work irresolute and cold;
34 *should be observed.*
Dilator, spe longus, iners, pavidusque futuri,
Difficilis, querulus, laudator temporis acti
Se puero, castigator censorque minorum.
Multa ferunt anni venientes commoda secum, 175
Multa recedentes adimunt. Ne forte seniles
Mandentur juveni partes pueroque viriles,
Semper in adjunctia sevoque morabimur aptis.
Aut agitur res in scenis, aut acta refertur.
Segniua irritant animos demissa per aurem, 180
Quani quse aunt oculis subjecta fidelibus, et quse
Ipse sibi tradit spectator. N"on tamen intus
Digna geri promes in scenam; multaque tolles

frigid style; a procrastinator, cherishing the hope of a prolonged existence, unex-citable and inactive, fearful and nervous about the future, peevish and testy, querulous, always praising the time that he spent when a hoy; the reprover and censor of those who ore his juniors. Ascending years bring many blessings and comforts with them ; declining years take many away. So that we must always pay careful attention to those circumstances which are connected with, and appropriate to, every age of human life, in order that the parts in the drama which belong to old men may not by any accident be intrusted to a young man, and that those which belong to a man may not be assigned to a boy.

An historical incident in the drama is either acted on the stage, or is related and described as having been transacted elsewhere. Things which are sent into the mind through the ear make a weaker impression upon our faculties and feelings than those which are submitted to the infallible testimony of sight, and which the spectator represents to himself *by teeing them with hit own eyet.* You will not, however, bring forward upon the stage things which are more fit for being enacted inside *and behind tin: scenes,* and you will remove much from the

Some Incidents should be 35
Postponing, long in hope, and sluggish, dull,
Of anxious fear of what may happen full;
Morose, complaining, always given to praise
The past experience of his boyish days;
Fond of . correcting and reproving all
Who, less in age, within his circle fall.
Years, as they flow, bring much to give us ease;
Years, as they ebb, take much that used to please.
Thus, as I said, we should with care observe 321
What suits each age, and thoughtfully preserve
For men the parts that men can act with truth,
Nor give the old the parts that suit the youth.
An action's either seen upon the stage,
Or else its story will our minds engage.
Things heard will much more languidly impress
Than those whose forms our faithful eyes address.
What the spectator sees, not what he's told,
His eyes, as witness to himself, behold. 330
Yet still you'll not expose to open view
What should be seen not even by a few:
36 *described, not represented.*
Ex oculis, qua mox narret facundia pnesens.
Ne pueros coram populo Medea trucidet; 185
Aut humana palam coquat exta nefarius Atreus ;
Aut in avem Progne vertatur, Cadmus in anguem.
Quodcunque ostendis mihi sic, incredulus odi.
Neve minor neu sit quinto productior actu
Fabula, quro posci vult et spoctata roponi; 190
Nec deus intersit, nisi dignus vindice nodus
Incident; nec quarta loqui persona laboret.
Actoris partes chorus officiumque virile
Defendat, neu quid medioa intercinet actus,
Quod' non proposito conducat et hsereat apte. 195

view of the audience which tho eloquence of an actor, supposed to have been present, can soon afterwards relate. Medea should not murder her sons before the people, nor should the impious Atreus cook his banquet of human entrails in the presence of the spectators, nor Progne be turned into a bird, nor Cadmus into a snake. Whatever you thus present to my view, I contemplate with feelings of incredulity and abhorrence.

A play should not be less than, nor extended beyond, five acts, which aims at being commanded, and after having been represented, to be performed again. Nor should a god interpose unless a perplexity should occur in the plot worthy of the aid of a god for its solution. Nor should a fourth character strive to speak in the same scene.

The chorus should sustain the parts of on actor, and an office in the drama, through its leader, as if it were a single performer, nor should it sing anything between the acts which does nofharmon- ise and appropriately correspond with the moral design of the

The Clwus sliould 37

Behind the stage there's much that may occur,
To which an actor can in time refer.
Let not Medea's butchery take place
Upon the boards before the public gaze;
Nor Atreus, impious and nefarious, there
His ghastly feast of human flesh prepare;
Nor Progne there a swallow's figure take,
Nor Cadmus within view become a snake. 340
Such scenes as these before the audience shown
I can't endure, but with disgust disown.
Into five acts, not less than five, you may,
Nor into more than five, divide your play;
A god should not step in with rules and laws,
When minor Solons can decide the cause ;
Nor should four persons speak in any scene,
If you desire your play to appear again.
The chorus should an actor's part sustain,
And do its duty like a single man, 350
And in its songs uphold the poet's aim,
The scope and purpose of its odes the same.
38 *advocate what is vIrtuous.*
Ille bonis faveatque et consilietur amice;
Et regat iratos, et amet peccare timentes;
Ille dapes laudet mensro brevis, ille saluhrem
Justitiam, legesque, et apertis otia portis;
Ille tegat commissa, Deosque precetur et oret 200
Ut redeat miseris, abeat fortuna superbis.

Tibia non, ut nunc, orichalco vincta, tubseque Emula, sed tenuis simplexque, foramine pauco, Adspirare et adesse choris erat utilis, atque Nondum spissa mmis complere sedilia flatu; 205 Quo sane populus numerabilis, utpote parvus Et frugi castusque verecundusque, coibat.

play. It should botl1 countenance tho goal, and give friendly advice; and exercise a control over tho passionate, and ehow u cordial approval of those who are afraid to sin ; it should commend the frugal meals of a short banquet; it should applaud salutary justice and obedience to the laws, and peace which is symbolised with open doors; it should conceal what is intrusted to it, and supplicate and implore the gods that fortune may return to the wretched and desert the proud.

The flute or flageolet, not such as it is now, embraced with ringft of mountain bronze, and rivalling the trumpet in sound and form, but low and slender in tone, and simple in its make, being constructed with only a few stops, was of use to accompany and assist the chorus, and to till with its sound the benches when they were not as yet too crowded, where the people, who could easily be counted, as being few in number, and who were of frugal and temperate habits, and of morally pure and untarnished manners, and modest in their demeanour, used to as-

On the Music of the Stage. . 39

It should applaud the virtuous, and it should '
Dispense such counsel as is kind and good,
Passion assuage, and those whom prudent fear
Restrains from sin, it should regard as dear;
A frugal meal, a temperate life commend,
The rules of honour and of truth defend ;
Champion of what is lawful, just, and right,
Of peace, whose gates are open day and night; 360
It should be faithful, and its prayers should rise,
That none should prosper but the good and wise ;
That fortune may desert the proud to bless
Those who're involved in undeserved distress.
The rustic flute, not that which now is bound
With rings of brass, and like the trump in sound,
But soft and simple, and with notes but few,
Used to assist and help the chorus to
Perform their part. Its tones, though feebly loud,
Could fill the house, in which a moderate crowd, 370
With ease computed, used at times to meet,
Frugal, correct, respectful, and discreet.

40 *The Alterations in*

Foatquam cujpit agros extendere victor, et urbem
Latior amplecti murus, vinoque diurno
Placari Genius festis impune diebus, 210
Accessit numerisque modisque licentia major.
Indoctus quid enim saperet liberque laborum
Rusticus urbano confusus, turpis honesto ?
Sic priscse motumque et luxuriem addidit arti
Tibicen, traxitque vagus per pulpita vestem. 215
Sic etiam fidibus voces crevere severis,
Et tulit eloquium insolitum facundia pweceps,
Utiliumque sagax rerum, et divina futuri,

humble. Afterwards, when the victorious Itonum began to extend hU territories, and a wider circuit of wall embraced thu city, und tlio presiding Genius was propitiated, without censure or restraint, with wine by day on festive occasions, a greater laxity and latitude were used in arranging the numbers of the poetry and the measures of the music. For what discerning or intelligent taste could be expected from such a motley audience, where thu countryman, uneducated and just set free from his laborious occupations, was indiscriminately seated in company with the polished citizen, and the man of debased character and degrading habits with the man of respectability and of honourable principles and conduct ? For this reason the musician added to his ancient art a more elaborate and lively style of melody, and u richness of harmony, and trailed a long robe after him as he paced up and down over the stage. Thus, too, notes were added to the solemn lyres used in tragedy, and an impetuous and unbridled style of diction in thu poet produced an unusual pomp of elocution in the actor, and the sentiment of the choric ode, quick in discerning and appreciating what is useful and expedient, and

the Flute and the Lyre. 41
Then when by conquest other lands were gained,
And Eome was by an ampler wall contained,
When wine was freely drunk on festive days,
The music and the poetry of plays
Received additions, that implied far more
Voluptuous licence than prevailed before.
For what nice taste could motley gatherings show,
Composed of high-bred men and rustics low, 380
Where, just released from toil, the illiterate clown
Sat with the man of noble style from town ?
Hence to their ancient art musicians joined
More brisk with richer harmonies combined,
And as they paced the comic boards around,
Trailed a long flowing mantle o'er the ground.
Thus, too, the grave and solemn tragic lyre
Did more, and loftier tones and notes acquire,
And gushing eloquence brought on the stage
Language unknown to any former age; 390
And in the chorus the pervading thought,
With moral wisdom useful lessons taught,
42 *On the Satyric Drama,*
Sortilegis non discrepuit sententia Delphis.
Carmine qui tragico vilem certavit ob hircum, 220
Mox etiam agrestes satyros nudavit, et asper
Incolumi gravitate jocum tentavit, eo quod
Illecebris erat et grata novitate morandus
Spectator, functusque sacris, et potus, et exlex.
Verum ita risores, ita commendare dicaces 225
Convenict satyros, ita vertere seria ludo,
Ne, quicunque deus, quicunque adhibebitur heros,
Regalj conspectus in auro nuper et ostro,
Migret in obscuras humili sermone tabernas,
Aut, dum vitat humum, nubes et inania captet. 230
Effutire leves indigna tragedia versus,
showing a prescience of the future, did not differ much from thu oracles of Delphi.

He who first contended in tragic verse for a worthless goat, soon exposed even rustic satyrs naked upon the stage, and sarcastically tried to be humorous and facetious while maintaining the grave and tragic character of his subject; for this reason, that the spectator had to be detained by exciting and sensational enticements, and by attractive and pleasing novelty, when he had finished his religious duties, and was stimulated by drink and regardless of all restraint. But it will be right so to introduce to the audience those laughing and diverting satyrs, so to manage the transition from what is serious to what is amusing, as that whatever god, whatever hero shall be brought forward, having been just seen conspicuously dressed out in regal gold and purple, shall not pass over into dark and dingy taverns, using mean and vulgar language in *the comic parts,* nor, while he avoids what is gross and grovelling, aspire to the clouds and to empty pomposities *in the tragic parts.* Tragedy, which disdains to babble out trivial verses as beneath her dignity, will, like a

and the Origin of it. 43
And warned with prescient ken almost divine,
Like the sage answers of the Delphic shrine.
He who contended first in tragic strain
For a vile goat, soon gave a loosened rein
To rude sarcastic jokes, and while he thought
Still to preserve a solemn style, he brought
Wild satyrs naked on the open stage,
By strange grotesque allurements to 'engage 400
The gazing crowd from sacred rites set free,
Inflamed with wine, and on. a reckless spree.
But if such sights as these can't be refused,
They should with strict propriety be used.
He who has just appeared to act the god,
In royal gold and purple richly clad,
Should not at once to some low tavern walk,
There to indulge in base degrading talk,
Nor, whilst he shuns such mean and grovelling speech,
Seek a vain pompous soaring style to reach. 410
The tragic goddess, who with pride disdains
To utter silly and licentious strains,
44 *Rules for its Management*
Ut festis matrona moveri jussa diebus,
Intererit satyris paulum pudibunda protervis.
Non ego inornata et dominantia nomina solum
Verbaque, Pisones, satyrorum scriptor amabo; 235
Nee sic enitar tragico differre colon,
Ut nihil intersit Davusne loquatur, et audax
Pythias, emuncto lucrata Simone talentum,
An custos famulusque dei Silenus alumni.
Ex noto fictum carmen sequar, ut sibi quivis 240
Speret idem, sudet multum frustraque laboret

Ausus idem : tantum series juncturaque pollet,

matron directed to dance on festive days, act amongst the wanton satyrs with some degree of modest decorum. I would not, Moon, as a writer of dramas in which satyrs are introduced, bo fond of using merely unembellished and commonly prevailing names and expressions ; nor would I Bo strive to deviate from the right complexion and character of tragedy as to make no difference whether a Davus is speaking, or a daring Pythias who has tricked and befooled Simo out of a talent, or Silenus, the care-taker and vulet of his pupil god. I would aim at composing a fictitious poem, taking my subject from some real and well-known occurrence, *and write in so natural a style and language* that any one might hope to do the same, but, when he was making the attempt, would labour much and exert himself to no purpose. So much does judicious arrangement and a nice combination of parts prevail, Bo much of excellence and ornament can be attached

and Style of Language. 45
Will act her part in a more comely way
'Mongst those who join in wild and wanton play;
Just as a matron, upon festive days,
When told to dance, with modesty obeys.
Were I satyric dramas to compose,
I would not use expressions mean and gross,
Devoid of ornament, and coarse and stale,
Such as 'mongst low and vulgar crowds prevail; 420
Nor would I strive to go so far away
From tragic style of language in my play,
As to make no distinction when a slave
Appears to speak, or Pythias badly brave,
Who has just choused old Simo of his gold,
Or Bacchus' guardian valet, *bald, and old.*
My plan is this : From some known fact I'll take
A theme from which fictitious odes I'll make,
And write that all might think they'd write as well,
But when they'd tried to write would surely fail. 430
So much can method and arrangement do,
So much ingenious combination too,
46 *On Versification:*
Tantum de medio sumptis accedit honoris.
Silvis deducti caveant, me judice, Fauni,
Ne, velut innati triviis, ac pene forenses, 245
Aut nimium teneris juvenentur versibus unquam,
Aut immunda crepent ignominiosaque dicta.
Offenduntur enim quibus est equus, et pater, et res;
Nee, si quid fricti ciceris probat et nucis emtor,
Equia accipitmt animis donantve corona. 250
Syllaba longa brevi subjecta vocatur iambus,
Pes citus; unde etiam trimetris accrescere jussit

Nomen iambeis, cum senos redderet ictus,
Primus ad extrenium aimilis sibi. Non ita pridem,
Tardior ut paulo graviorque veniret ad aures, 255
Spondeos atabiles in jura paterna recepit

to subjects derived from an ordinary source or from the transactions of common life. Fauns taken from the woods should, in my opinion, be careful neither to play off their juvenile sports in too refined and delicate strains, like those who have been born in the city, and almost like persons connected with the forum, nor gabble out obscene and disgraceful expressions; for those who possess an equipage, and an ancestry, and an estate, are disgusted ; nor, if the purchaser of parched vetches and nuts approves of anything of this kind, do they acknowledge it with satisfaction, or confer upon such actors the laurel crown,

A long syllable put next to a short one is called an iambus – a quick measure. Whence also it ordered the desi gnation of trimeters to be given to iambics, even though the iambic line answered to six beats, each foot being the same from lii.-t to lost. Not long ago, in order that the verse might reach the ear with a more deliberate and majestically solemn tone, it received the steady spondees into a share of its paternal rights, with kind and

Mixture of Iambics and Spondees. 47
So much of beauty, elegance, and grace
Can be impressed on themes, though commonplace.
Fauns that are brought from woods should seek with care
Not to disport with soft and tender air,
Like loungers in the streets and public ways,
Nor chatter filthy and disgusting lays ;
For they who style and rank and wealth possess
Are shocked to witness such unseemliness ; 440
Nor, though the man who deals with hucksters smiles
At acting which his paltry care beguiles,
Can noble critics grant the laurel crown
To those whose actings only cause a frown.
When a long syllable to a short is joined,
Tis an iambus, rapid in its sound;
Hence on iambic lines, of beats though six,
The name of trimeters it chose to fix.
Not long ago, to give a slower sound,
And make the verse send forth a tone profound, 450
With kind concession and with friendly care,
On solid spondees it conferred a share

48 *The Romans bad Judges*
Commodus et patiens ; non nt de sede secunda
Cederet aut quarta socialiter. Hie et in Acci
Nobilibus trimetris apparet rarus, et Enni
In scenam missos magno cum pondere versus, 260
Aut opera celeris nimium curaque carentis,

Aut ignoratse premit artis crimiue turpi.

Non quivis videt immodulata potimata judcx : Et data Romanis venia est indigna poetis. Idcircone vager, scribamque licenter, ut omnes 265 Visuros peccata putem mea, tutus et intra Spem venise cautus ? Vitavi denique culpam,

patient acquiescence, but with a sociable stipulation that it was not to withdraw from the second and fourth position in the line. This kind of measure is seldom met with in the much-applauded trimeters of Accius, and *tlie absence of it* brands the verses of Ennius, launched upon the stage with an oppressive weight of spondees, with the reproach of their being either the result of a too hasty and slovenly execution, or of his being ignorant of the art of versification.

It in not every critic who perceives incorrectly modulated verses, and *consequently* an unworthy and undeserved indulgence is granted to Roman poets. Shall I, therefore, carelessly ramble and write without attending to the rules of prosody, although *[* should suppose that even all would perceive my faults, feeling safe and cautious to the extent of keeping within hope of pardon *]*

of Smooth Versification. 49

Of its paternal rights, reserving still

Its claim the second and fourth place to fill.

This style of measure is but seldom found

In the trimctric lines of boasted sound

Which Accius wrote, and Ennius who sent

His verses on the stage with proud intent,

In which a cumbrous weight of spondees proves

That his inventive skill too swiftly moves, 460

Or that the care he used was far too small,

Or that he did not know his art at all.

Not every judge has science to detect Poems of tone untuned and incorrect, And Roman poets are allowed to speak With an indulgence they should scorn to seek. Shall I then ramble and at random write, Though I should deem my faults exposed to sight, Safe in the hope that I'm from censure free, If this indulgence be allowcd to me ? 470

Cautious so far, at best I'm free from blame,

But have not earned a poct's praise or fame.

50 *The Progress of*

Noijl laudem merui. Vos exemplaria Grasca

Nocturna versato manu, versate diurna.

At vestri proavi Plautinos et numeros et 270

Laudavere sales; nimium patienter utrumque,

Ne dicam stulte, mirati; si modo ego et vos

Scimus inurbanum lepido seponere dicto,

Legitimumque sonum digitis callemus et auro.

Ignotum tragicJc genus invenisse camenro 275

Dicitur, et plaustris vexisse poemata Thespis

Qui canerent agerentque peruncti facibus ora.

Post hunc, persone pallseque repertor honestaj

jEschylus, et modicis instravit pulpita tignis,

In that case I have at best avoided censure, I have not merited praise.

Do you carefully examine and study by night and day the models which Grecian poets have left us. Yet your ancestors praised both the numbers and witticisms of Plautus, admiring both with a too submissive and acquiescent feeling of approval, I will not say with an absurdity of admiration, if only I and you know how to distinguish an"inelegant expression from one of genuine facetiousness, and have skill to recognise and appreciate with our fingers and ears a sound that complies with the laws of harmonious versification.

Thespis is said to have invented a description of tragedy , till then unknown, and to have brought about in waggons men who sang and acted his poetical compositions, having their faces daubed over with lees of wine. After him jEschylus, the inventor of the mask, and of the becoming and respectable-looking mantle, both covered over the place for acting with some moderate-sized planks, and taught the-

the Greek Drama. 51

The standard models Greece has left, by night,
By day, explore them, ye who wish to write.
Yet your too partial ancestors have thought
Worthy of praise the rhymes that Plautus wrote:
Looking too calmly, I don't wish to say
With too much folly, on his sportive lay;
If I may but assume that I and you
Have taste to know coarse wit from what is true,
And can decide with fingers and with ears 481
What sounds correct, and what uncouth appears.

The first to try a novel tragic art Was Thespis, who, in rude and rustic cart, Carried his actors all the country through, Their faces smeared with lees of purple hue. Next after him did Eschylus invent The comely mask and, with polite intent, The robe that covered his performers when He wished to'make them look like well-dressed men. ; -.

JtV"""" He made a stage with scanty planks, and taught 491 &
His men to speak their parts in language fraught

62 Roman Writers have failed

Et docuit magnumque loqui, nitique cothurno. 280
Successit vetus his comoedia, non sine multa
Laude; sed in vitium libertas excidit et vim
Dignam lege regi. Lex est accepta, chorusque
Turpiter obticuit, sublato jure nocendi.
Nil intentatum nostri liquere poeto: 285
Nee minimum meruere decus vestigia Gneca
Ausi deserere et celebrare domestica facta,
Vel qui pratextas, vel qui docuere togatas.
Nec virtute foret clarisve potentius armis
Quam lingua Latium, si non oflenderet unum – 290
Quemque poetarum limss labor et mora. Vos, 0

performers to speak in loud and lofty language, and to strut, about in the buskin. Ancient comedy came in next "after these, not without much applause ; but the freedom it allowed degenerated into vicious excess, and into an uncontrollable licentiousness, which it was right to have regulated by legal enactment. A law was passed and submitted to, and the chorus having been deprived of the power of injuring by its slanders, to its disgrace became silent.

Our poets have left no kind of dramatic composition un- attempted ; nor have they deserved least honour who have had the courage to abandon the custom of following in the footsteps . of the Grecians, and to commemorate the achievements of their own country, either those who have instructed actors in tragedies or in comedies. Nor would Italy have been more famous and influential on account of her heroism and illustrious achievements in war, than by her literature, if the toil and delay of I correcting and revising did not act as a stumbling-block to every lone of our poets. Do you, who are of the noble blood of Numa

from not Correcting tlteir Works. 53

With stately tone and pompous style of talk,
And on the boards in tragic buskin stalk.
Next after these old comedy appeared,
And by applauding multitudes was heard;
But when the rule of libel it transgressed,
By stringent law its freedom was suppressed.
Then when the chorus could no more defame,
Twas basely silent, and extinct became. 500

Our poets have to all their minds applied And left no form of poetry untried. Nor should we fail to give due praise to those Who tragic verse or comic strains compose, Who've boldly ceased through Grecian tracks to roam, To seek their facts and incidents at home. Nor would our country bear a prouder name For great achievements and for martial fame, Than a grand place in future history fill With fame for learning and dramatic skill, ' 51 o If our poetic writers would but choose The file with care and frequency to use.

54 *An Affectation of Genius*

Pompilius sanguis, carmen reprehendite, quod non
Multa dies et multa litura coercuit, atque
Prsesectum decies non castigavit ad unguem.
Ingenium misera quia fortunatius arte 295
Credit, et excludit sanos Helicone poetas
Democritus, bona pars non ungues ponere curat,
Non barbam; secrota petit loca, balnea vitat.
Nanciscetur enim pretium nomenque poetse,
Si tribus Anticyris caput insanabile nunquam 300
Tonsori Ldcino commiserit. 0 ego Iibvus,
Qui purgor bilem sub verni temporis horam!
Non alius faceret meliora poemata. Verum

Pompilius, pass a verdict of censure upon that poem which much time and many erasures have not pruned and corrected over and over again, Bo that the most sensitive and fastidious taste cannot detect a blemish, just as the nicely-cut nail of the artist cannot discern the slightest inequality on the well-polished surface of a marhle sjab.

Because Democritus believes that natural genius is more successful than application and study, which he despises as wretched and pitiful, and excludes from Helicon all who are sane and sensible, a considerable *number of self-constituted poets* are careless about cutting their nails or their beard: they search for secret haunts, they avoid the baths ; for they imagine that they shall acquire the reputation and title of poet if they have never intrusted their heads, which three Anticyrre could not cure, to thu barber Licinus 1 Oh, perverse and stupid man that I am ! who got rid of my bile at the approach of spring. *Otherurise* no one else could make better poems ! But nothing is worth to great

leads to Absurdity. 55

Do you, my noble friends, that work reject
Which length of time and toil did not correct,
And make so finished that the critic's eye
Can scarce a single blot or blemish spy;
Like the smooth slab on which you'll seek in vain
A flaw to mar its finely polished plane.
Because Democritus propounds the creed
That genius without art is all we need, 520
And will not let a poet who is sane
Do homage in the Muses' mountain fane,
Nor drink the draughts which Helicon supplies
To fill his mind with fancies bright and wise,
Your would-be poets think that nails grown long
And beards unshaved denote a taste for song;
They seek retirement, from the baths they run,
With thrice mad brain the barbers' razors shun..
Ah mo I regardless of this golden rule,
Who ne'er was taught in this romantic school, 530
Could I in spring-time but retain my bile,
I'd be a poet of surpassing style.

56 *Good Sense is the*

Nil tanti est. Ergo fungar vice cotis, acutum
Keddere quro ferrum valet, exsors ipsa secandi: 305
Munus et officium, nil scribens ipse, docebo;
Unde parentur opes; quid alat formetque poetam;
Quid deceat, quid non; quo virtus, quo ferat error.
Scribendi recte sapere est et principium et fons:
Eem tibi Socraticse poterunt ostendere chartaj; 310
Verbaque provisam rem non invita sequentur.
Qui didicit patriro quid debeat, et quid amicis;
Quo sit amore parens, quo frater amandus et hospes,

a price *as to pay your mi nit y of mind for it.* I will therefore perform the office of a whetatone, which can render the iron instrument sharp, while the stone itself is incapable of cutting. While I write nothing myself, I will give instructions as to the duty and office *of a good writer;* whence materials are procured ; what improves and makes the poet; what is suitable and graceful, and what is not so ; to what a right knowledge and appreciation of the essential beauty of genuine poetry, or a misconception of its requirements, may lead.

Qood sense is the elementary basis and originating source of good writing. The literary productions of those ethical writers who have adopted the philosophical system of Socrates will be able to suggest to you a subject; and when your selected subject has been well considered and digested, words will not unwillingly but spontaneously follow. He who has learned what he owes to his country, and what to his friends, with what amount of affectionate attachment a parent, or a brother, or a visitor is to

Foundation of Good Writing. 57
But the distinction is not worth the pay,
I therefore choose a far superior way :
The grindstone's office I shall seek to do,
Which cannot cut, but makes the knife cut through;
And while I do not write, I'll strive to teach
The poet's art to all within my reach ;
Whence rich material and resources flow,
What forms the poet and what makes him grow, 540
What gives a seemly air and what does not,
What merit can effect, and failure what.
Good, sound, judicious sense with taste combined
Is the grand spring in a good writer's mind.
Of subject-matter you can have a store
In the rich records of Socratic lore;
And when your theme by previous thought you know,
Words will come forth in smooth spontaneous flow.
He who has learned what generous deeds are due
To his own country, to his kindred too; 550
What friendships claim, what filial loves demand,
In what esteem should guests or brothers stand ;
58 *A Study of Ethics Illustrated*
Quod sit con scrip ti, quod judicis officium, quse
Partes in bellum missi ducis, ille profecto 315
Eeddere persons e scit convenientia cuique.
Respicere exemplar vitse morumque jubebo
Doctum imitatorem, et vivas bine ducere voces.
Interdum speciosa locis morataque recto
Fabula, nullius veneris, sine pondere et arte, 320
Valdius oblectat populum, meliusque moratur,
Quam versjls inopes rerum nugseque canorse.
Graiis ingenium, Graiis dedit ore rotundo
Musa loqui, prater laudem nullius avaris.
be regarded ; what is the duty of a senator, what of a judge ;

what are the proper functions of a general sent to conduct a
war; that man undoubtedly knows how to attribute to each
character what is suitable and appropriate. My direction to
the dramatic writer who is thus well instructed is this – to
look back upon an original standard of real life and manners to
guide him in the *delineation of his character,* and, from a con-
templation of this, to derive descriptive language, which will
be instinct with reality, *and which will represent his portraits to
the life.* Sometimes a dramatic story, which contains striking
and attractive incidents, and in which the manners and characters are well portrayed, but which is of no genuine beauty, and
which is destitute of elegance of style and of solidity of diction,
and of artistic arrangement, more effectually delights a popular
audience, and has better success in keeping up their attention,
than well-composed verses characterised by a poverty of matter
and of moral sentiment, and which are merely fine-sounding
trifles.

To the Greeks, ambitious
of nothing but glory, the Muse has given genius ; to the Greeks she has given
the ability to express themselves in a smoothly flowing and tersely rounded style of
speech. The young men

by Living Examples is Essential. 59
What rule should guide the man who makes our laws,
And by what rule the judge decide a cause ;
How should the. general act when sent to wield
His glittering sword upon the battle-field;
That man knows how, by wisdom sound and true,
To assign to each, to each what's rightly due.
In real life his thus instructed mind .'
A model safe, correct, and just can find; 560
When his conceptions shall with this agree,
Then true to nature will his language be.
Sometimes a tale made up of topics fine,
With morals well brought out in every line,
Though without elegance, or strength, or art,
Charms with much more delight the listener's heart,
Than well-spun verses wanting solid thought,
And though harmonious, yet with trifles fraught.

Transcendent genius, and a power to speak With polished grace, the Muse has given
the Greek, And the sole passion Grecian minds could raise 571 Was love of glory and
undying praise.

60 *Why the Grecians write*
Eomani pueri longis rationibus assem 325
Discunt in partes centum diducere. Dicat
Filius Albini, Si de quincunce remota est

Uncia, quid superet ? Poteras dixisse; Triens. Eu !
Eem poteris servare tuam. Eedit uncia, quid fit ?
Semis. At, hsec animos serugo et cura peculi 330
Cum semel imbuerit, speramus carmina fingi
Posse linenda cedro et levi servanda cupresso ?
Aut prodesse volunt, aut delectare poetse,
Aut simul et jucunda et idonea dicere vitse.
Quidquid prsecipies, esto brevis, ut cito dicta 335
Percipiant animi dociles, teneantque fideles :
Omno supervacuum pleno de pectoro manat .

of Home, *on the other Iwnd,* learn by long calculations to divide an as into a
hundred parts. Let the son of Albinus tell this: "If from a quincunx (or five unciio)
an uncia he taken, what remains?" You could have said, " A triens (or four ounces,
the third part of an as)." " Ah ! very good 1 You will have arithmetical knowledge
enough to enable you to manage your own property with economy. Now add an uncia;
what is the result]" "A semis (six ounces, or half of an as)." But when this corroding
anxiety and concern about paltry riches has once pervaded and saturated their mental
faculties, do we expect that verses can be composed by them worthy to be covered
over with oil of cedar, and to be i kept securely deposited in cases of polished cypress
?

Poets have it as their object either to give instruction or to give pleasure, or to give
expression at the same time to what is pleasing and to what is serviceable for the
management of life. Whatever you write in the didactic style, or for moral teaching,
let it be brief and sententious; that the minds of those whom you wish to instruct
may at once perceive with docility, and retain with fidelity, what you say. Everything
superfluous or redundant flows away

belter than tfte Romans. 61
Our Roman youths, with arithmetic pride,
Learn by long rules a penny to divide .
Into a hundred parts. Albums' son
Is told to solve, and bring this problem done :
" If from five ounces just an ounce you takc,
What difference will it by subtraction make ? "
" Why, four remain." " Ah I right my boy! I see
You'll hold your own, and save an agent's fee. 580
Now add an ounce, and the sum total fix."
" Then the sum total will amount to six."
When this corroding, cankering greed for gain
Absorbs the affections and the mind, 'tis vain
To hope for verses worthy f a place,
Preserved with cedrium, in a cypress case.
All poets wish to profit or delight,
Or to combine the two in what they write.
Let moral precepts bo concise and plain,
What minds can soon perceive and well retain. 590

All that's superfluous in what you say,
From the full breast and memory flows away.
Poems should Combine
Ficta voluptatis causa sint proxima veris :
Nee quodcunque volet poscat sibi fabula credi;
Neu pransro Lamise vivum puerum extrahat alvo. 340
Centurise seniorum agitant expertia frugis; Celsi pretereunt austera poemata Ramnes.
Omne tulit punctum qui miscuit utile dulci, Lectorem delectando pariterque monendo.
Hie meret sera liber Sosiis; hie et mare transit, 345 Et longum noto scriptori prorogat
sevum.
Sunt delicta tamen, quibus ignovisse velimus: Nam neque chorda sonum reddit
quem vult manus et mens, Poscentique gravem perssepe remittit acutum ;

from a full memory. Fictitious representations which are intended to give pleasure
should border as nearly as possible upon what is real; nor should your play demand
credence for whatever improbabilities it shall wish to advance ; nor, *for example,*
should it extract a living boy from the stomach of Lamia after she had feasted on him.

The centuries of senators reject productions which are devoid of mural instruction.
Exalted knights disregard poetical compositions which are grave and dry. He has
gained every vote who has combined the useful with the agreeable, by contributing
to the entertainment of his reader, and in the same degree giving him admonitory and
beneficial instruction. A book of this kind makes money for the publishers ; this also
crosses the sea, to be read in foreign countries, and extends a protracted duration of
glory to its distinguished author.

There are faults, however, to which we may be inclined to extend indulgence.
For neither does the string always send forth the exact tone which the hand and the
intention of the player desire, and very frequently it returns a sharp note when he
requires a flat; nor will

Instruction with Entertainment. 63
Fictions intended to give pleasure ought
To be like truths and real actions wrought.
Let not your play require us to believe
All the strange things your fancy may conceive –
That of a boy a sorceress made a feast,
And then disgorged him – injured not the least I
What won't instruct, grave senators reject;
Poems too solemn, stately knights neglect. 600
He will obtain the votes of all with ease,
Who blends the useful with what's sure to please.
In him the reader will amusement find,
0
As well as moral culture for his mind.
A book like this brings profit, and repays
The author's toil with European praise;
This into future years prolongs his name,
And crowns his memory. with immortal fame.

Yet there are faults to which we'd fain extend
The fair indulgence of a candid friend. 610
Just as the string stretched on the pleasant harp,
When we require a flat, emits a sharp;
64 *Faults in Poetry. which*
Nec semper feriet quodcunque minabitur arcus. 350
Verum ubi plura nitent in carmine, non ego paucis
Offendar maculis, quas aut incuria fudit,
Aut humana parum cavit natura. Quid ergo est ?
Ut scriptor si peccat idem librarius usque,
Quamvis est monitus, venia caret; et citharoedus 355
Ridetur, chorda qui semper oberrat eadem:
Sic mihi, qui multum cessat, fit Chcerilus ille,
the bow always strike whatever is aimed at. ' But when the bright points in a poem
constitute the majority, I will not be offended by a few blemishes, which either B
slight negligence has caused, or which the ability of human nature has not sufficiently.
guarded against. What then) *how doei the cote stand f* Just as tho transcriber, if he
constantly commits the same mistakes, although he has been admonished, forfeits
all claim to forbearance, and as the harper becomes a laughing-stock who always
blunders on the same string, thus the man who makes many mistakes in his attempts
at poetical composition, becomes, to my view, a sort of
may be overlooked. 65
And as the bow won't always strike its aim,
A poet's luck is often much the same.
But when more bright attractive beauties shine
Than the few spots in some occasional line,
I'm not the uncandid critic to condemn
The aspiring author to the blush of shame,
When but the want of nice fastidious care
Has left the slight and trifling blemish there, 620
Or the perfection hc would gladly reach
Defies the grasp of human taste or speech.
What then ? you'll say; where do you draw the lino
Between what's blamcablc and what is fine ?
Ill tell you that: just as the man you ask
To write or copy an appointed task,
If he the same mistakes too oft repeats,
Although admonished, no indulgence meets ;
And as the harper only makes you smile,
Who always harps in one discordant style, 630
So does the poet who goes much astray
Become to me a Choerilus, who may
66 *Poetry is like Painting.*
Quem bis terve bonum cum risu miror; et idem
Indignor quandoque bonus dormitat Homerus.

Verum operi longo fas est obrepere somnum. 360
Ut pictura, poesis : erit quse, si proprius stes,
Te capiet magis, et qusedam, si longius abstes:
Hroc amat obscurum; volet heec sub luce videri,
Judicis argutum quso non formidat acumen;
ILcc placuit semel, hajc decies repetita placebit. 365
0 major juvenum, quamvis et voce paterna Fingeris ad rectum, et per te sapis, hoc tibi dictum Tolle memor, – certis medium et tolerabile rebus Eecte concedi. Consultus juris et actor Causarum mediocris abest virtute diserti 370

Choorilus, at whom, if he is tolerably good in two or three instances, I express surprise with laughter ; and I, the very same man, am provoked and annoyed whenever Homer, who really deserves the title of good, becomes drowsy. But it is allowable that sleepiness should occasionally creep upon the author who is engaged in a long work.

Poetry is like painting. There will be some piece which, if you stand nearer, will gain your attention the more, and some if you stand at a greater distance. This courts the shade; this will desire to be seen near the light, which does not dread the discriminating penetration of a good judge. This has pleased once; this, though repeated ten times, will still give pleasure.

Do you, who are the elder of my young friends, – although you are trained and moulded to what is right by your father's instruction, and of yourself have a wise faculty of discernment – receive and remember this as my verdict, that for some things a middling and passable degree of excellence is rightly conceded. A man who is consulted on legal matters, and who is but a moderate advocate, may be far from the merit of the eloquent Messala, nor

Mediocrity cannot be 67
Twice or three times produce what's fit for view,
Causing amazement and amusement too.
And when good worthy Homer droops away,
I feel indignant in a friendly way.
Yet in a work that's long 'tis hard to keep,
Throughout the entire, completely free from sleep.
Poems are as paintings: some will strike your eye With more effect far off, and some if nigh. 640
This loves the shade, another asks for light,
Which does not dread the critic's piercing sight.
This has pleased once, and this will please again,
'Twill please although repeated ten times ten.
I now address my elder friend alone,
Although paternal counsel gives a tone
To your judicious mind, yet hear from-me
And store this maxim in your memory; –
In some professions we can reconcile
Our minds to mediocrity of style. 650
i
A lawyer, who is moderately fit

To plead a client's cause, may want the wit
68 *tolerated in Poetry.*

Messalro, nec scit quantum Cascellius Aulus; Sed tamen in pretio est: mediocribus esse poetis . Non homines, non dl, non concessere columnse. Ut gratas inter mensas symphonia discors, 374

Et crassum unguentum, et Sardo cum melle papaver
. Ofibndunt, potorat duci quia coena sine istis;
Sic animis natum inventumque poema juvandis,
Si paulum summo decessit, vergit ad imum.

Ludere qui nescit campestribus abstinet ermis, Indoctusque pilro discive trochive quiescit, 380

Ne spissro risum tollant impune coronse:
Qui nescit, versus tamen audet fingere! Quidni ?

doe? he know as much of Law as Cascellius Aulus, yet still he ia held in estimation ; but neither men, nor gods, nor booksellers' shops, have allowed that poets should be middling. As at agreeable entertainments, discordant music, and thick perfume, and poppy with Sardinian honey, are offensive, because the banquet might have been conducted without these *affected luxuries;* so poetical compositions, produced and contrived for giving pleasure to our minds, if they have only deviated a little from the highest utanduj-d of excellence, sink towards the lowest.

He who knows not how to take part in the games, abstains from the arms and athletic instruments used in the Campus Martius ; and he who is not instructed in the use of the ball, or the quoit, or the hoop, remains quiet, lest the surrounding crowds should justly raise a laugh against him. Yet he who knows nothing of the Art of Poetry, has the presumption to make verses ! Why not *I* He is a freeman ami nobly born, especially

Necessity for Study . 69
Of eloquent Messala, who has skill
The forum with applauding crowds to fill,
Nor may he know what Aulus knows, a man
Who every form and phase of law can scan;
Yet he's esteemed, and holds an honoured place
In his profession with becoming grace;
But that a poet should be middling now,
Nor men nor gods nor publishers allow. 660
As ill-tuned music at a welcome feast,
And coarse and thick perfume., offend the taste,
And poppy mixed with honey that *is* bad
Impairs the pleasure that might else be had;
So poems that should please, if they descend
From a high standard, to the lowest tend.

He who knows nothing of the bold exploits Played in the parks with balls and hoops and quoits, Abstains from joining, lest the wondering crowd Should justly roar with laughter long and loud; 670 Yet he presumes to publish verses still, Who has nor genius nor poetic skill !

70 *and Diligent Correcting.*

Liber et ingenuus, pnEsertim' census equestrem
Summam nummorum, vitioque remotus ab omni.
Tu nihil invita dices faciesve Minerva: 385
Id tibi judicium est, ea mens. Si quid tamen olim
Scripseris, in Mseci descendat judicis aures,
Et patris, et nostras, nonumque prematur in annum,
Membranis intus positis. Delete licebit
Quod non edideris; nescit vox missa reverti. 390
Silvestres homines sacer interpresque deorum Csedibus et victu foedo deterruit
Orpheus ; Dictus ob hoc lenire tigres rabidosque leones. Dictus et Amphion, Thebame
conditor arcis, Saxa movere sono testudinis, et prece blanda 395

he is rated at an equestrian amount of money, and fur removed from every vice.
You will say or do nothing if Minerva should be unpropitious. Such is your judgment,
such is your resolution. If, however, you shall hereafter write anything, let it bo
submitted to the hearing of Meecius as a judge of it, and to your fathers, and to my
critical inspection, and let it be suppressed for nine yean, your manuscripts being
safely deposited out of the reach of public observation. You will have power to erase
what you have not published. A word once sent forth can never return.

Orpheus, the priest and interpreter of the gods, made uncivilised men abstain from
bloodshed and savage diet; so that he was reputed, on this account, to have tamed
tigers and raging lions. Amphion also, the builder of the Thcban citadel, was said to
move stones by the sound of his lyre, and by soothing

A Eidogium on the Dignity of Poetry. 71

Why not ? He's nobly born, and rich, and free
From vices which in other men we see.
I feel convinced you'll nothing say or do
Unless you find Minerva kind and true.
Such is your judgment, such your sound intent;
Yet if on writing you should still be bent,
Submit to Msecius or your father's sight,
Or show to me the verses that you write, 680
And keep them back, laid by for nine full years,
Till they can please our sharp fastidious ears.
What you've not published you can change it all;
A word once published is beyond recall.
Orpheus first tamed the savage human throng
By the enchantments of his sacred song,
Taught men from bloody carnage to abstain,
And from polluted diet to refrain :
Hence in historic legends he was famed
Tigers and raging lions to have tamed. 690
Amphion too, who built the Theban wall,
Put stones in motion by the alluring call

72 *On the Benefits Poetry*

Ducere quo vellet. Fuit hsec sapientia quondam,
Publica privatis secernere, sacra profanis,
Concubitu prohibere vago, dare jura maritis,
Oppida moliri, leges incidere ligno.
Sic honor et nomen divinis vatibus atque 400
Carminibus venit. Post hos insignis Homerus,
Tyrticusquo mares animos in martia bella
Versibus exacuit; dictaj per carmina sortes,
Et vitse monstrata via est, et gratia regum

allurements to lead them wherever he wished. This was wisdom *on the part ofpoeU* in former ages, to show the distinction between public and private interests, between sacred things and things profane, to restrain from licentious intercourse between the sexes, to give laws to the married, to plan cities, to engrave legal enactments in wood. Thus glory and reputation redounded to divine poets and to their poetical productions. After these, renowned Homer and Tyrtoras incited manly spirits to martial achievements by their verses. Oracles were delivered in verse. And the proper course of life was pointed out, and the favour of

has conferred on Man. 73
Of his enchanting lyre, and led them where
He pleased to bring them by enticing prayer.
In former ages poets used their art
Lessons of moral wisdom to impart,
Taught men the prudent means by which they should
Distinguish private from the public good;
How to know sacred things from things profane,
And from all vague promiscuous loves abstain. 700
Poets gave rules to those in wedded life,
To teach the husband and instruct the wife.
Towns were constructed, laws were carved in wood,
While poets as presiding patrons stood.
Thus did the poet and his verses shine
With fame and honour you might call divine.
Next after these imperial Homer came,
Tyrtoeus too, in verses to proclaim
What praise in war, what glory can be gained,
Through martial deeds by manly minds sustained.
In verse the gods declared their will to man: 711
In verse was shown the safe and moral plan
74 *Nature and Art must*
t
Pieriis tentata modis, ludusque repcrtus, 405
Et longorum operum finis: ne forte pudori
Sit tibi Musa lyne solers, et cantor Apollo.
Natura fieret laudabile carmen, an arte,
- Quajsitum est. Ego nee studium sine divite vena,

Nee rude quid possit video ingenium: alterius sic 410

Altera poscit opem res et conjurat amice.

Qui studet optatam curau contingere metam, Multa tulit fecitque puer, sudavit et alsit, Abstinuit venere et vino; qui Pythia cantat'

kings was solicited in Pierian measures, and games were introduced and commemorated, and the termination of tedious labours was celebrated in verse. So do not allow the muse who is skilled in the lyre, nor Apollo, the god of song, to cause you a blush.

It has been made a subject of inquiry whether a poem worthy of being commended ia composed as the result of natural talent or of art . I neither sec what study, without a rich vein of natural genins, nor what genius, in its primitive state and uncultivated, can effect . Thus each requires to have the assistance of the other, and both combine amicably *for the same end.*

The man who exerts himself to reach the desired goal in the race, has endured and done much in the way of practice from the time of his boyhood; has perspired with heat, and suffered cold; lias abstained from improper indulgences and from wine. The musician who sings the Pythian songs was first a learner, and feared

Combine to form a Poet. 75

Of life : and kings were asked in verse to grant

Whatever favours they who asked might want.

Games were described and patronised in song;

Poems gave pleasure after toils too long:

So do not let the muse that tunes the lyre,

Nor let the god who gives poetic fire,

And binds tlie poet's brow with wreaths of fame,

Cause you a moment's blush or tinge of shame. 720

It has been asked, Does nature or does art

Poetic talent to the mind impart ?

My voice is this, that neither study can

Succeed without a rich poetic vein,

Nor that great genius, unless cultured well,

Can in poetic composition tell:

Thus each requires to have the other's aid,

By both combined a good result is made.

He who aspires the wished-for prize to gain

In the swift race upon Olympia's plain, . 730

Has toiled in practice, suffered cold and heat,

Abstained from pleasures, sober and discreet;

76 Rich Amateur Poets

Tibicen, didicit prius extimuitque magistrum. 415 Nunc satis est dixisse, " Ego mira poemata pango; Occupet extremum scabies; mihi turpe relinqui est, Et quod non didici sane nescire fateri."

Ut prseco, ad merces turbam qui cogit emendas, Assentatores jubet ad lucrum ire poeta 420

Dives agris, dives positis in fenore nummis.

Si vero est unctum qui recto ponere possit,

Et spondere levi pro paupere, et eripere atris
Litibus implicitum, mirabor si sciet inter-
Noscere mendacem verumque beatus amicum. 425
Tu, seu donaris seu quid donare voles cui,
Nolito ad versus tibi factos ducere plenum
a master. Now it in enough to have said, " I muko wonderful poems. Let a plague
seize the hindmost. For me it is disgraceful to be left behind, and, in fact, to confess
that I am ignorant of what I have never learned."

As the auctioneer collects a crowd to buy his goods, Bo a poet who is rich in lands,
rich in money laid out at usury, invites obsequious auditors to come to a rehearsal of
his poetry for their own gain. But if he is a person who can serve up a splendid banquet
in correct style, and can be security for a poor man who has no credit himself, and
who can rescue a man who is embarrassed by dismal lawsuits, I shall feel astonished
if he shall have the good fortune to know the difference between a false and n true
friend. I advise you, whether you have conferred a gift or shall wish to confer a gift
upon any one, not to bring him to hear verses made by you when he is full of delight
at your generosity;

Cautioned against Flatterers, 77
He who desires the Pythian airs to sing,
Has learned the skill which art and lessons bring;
Now 'tis enough to say, " I write grand verse;
I core not who's behind or who writes worse;
That I should be surpassed, for me 'twere base,
And though untaught to acknowledge this" disgrace."
Just as the crier lures the passing crowd
To buy his wares, a poet rich and proud 740
Invites all those he thinks disposed to praise,
To hear for gain his loved poetic lays.
But if he can a sumptuous feast dispense,
And bail a debtor at his own expense,
If he can save him from the griping claws,
Coiling around him, of extracting laws,
I'll be surprised if that man can attend
To know a flatterer from a genuine friend.
'Tis my advice if you intend to show
Some liberal kindness to a man you know, . 750
Let him not come when full of joy to hear
Verses from which he can't withhold a cheer.
78 *and their Insincere*
Lsetitise: clamabit enim, " Pulchre ! Bene ! Eecte !"
Pallescet super his; etiam stillabit amicis
Ex oculis rorem; saliet, tundet pede terram. 430
Ut quse conducti plorant in funere, dicunt
Et faciunt prope plura dolentibus ex animo, sic
Derisor vero plus laudatore movetur.

Eeges dicuntur multis urgere culullis,
Et torquere mero quem perspexisse laborant, 435
An sit amicitia dignus: si carmina condes,
Nunquam te fall ant animi sub vulpe latentes.
Quintilio si quid recitares, " Corrige, sodes,
Hoc," aiebat, " et hoc." Melius te posse negares,
Bis torque exportum frustra, delere jubebat, 440
Et malo tornatos incudi reddero versus.
Si defendere delictumi quam vortere, malles,

for he will exclaim, " Admirable ! excellent! how correct!" He will grow pale in addition to uttering these exclamations. He will even drop tears of dewy moisture from his friendly eyes, lie will leap about; he will beut the ground with his foot . As those who utter lamentations for hire at a funeral say and do nearly more than those who grieve from the heart, so the hypocritical applauder is more visibly affected than the man who tenders sincere praise. Kings are said to ply with many cups, and to rack with wine, a man whom they wish thoroughly to see if he is worthy of their friendship. . If you will compose verses, never let treacherous thoughts, lying concealed under the guise of a cunning and hypocritical countenance and attitude, deceive you. If you recited anything to Quintilius, lie would sny, " Correct, if you please, this, and this." If you should tell him that you could not possibly do better, having made the attempt two or three times without success, he would desire you to blot out, and again to submit to the anvil your badly constructed verses. If you preferred to defend rather than to correct a fault, he would

and Fulsome Praise. 79
" Well done," he'll cry; " how nobly he can write !"
He's all enraptured with assumed delight;
Pale with surprise, his eyes distil a few
Drops of most friendly eulogising dew :
He'll leap and stamp. As mourners hired to cry
Say and do more than ge'nuine mourners nigh,
So a false friend, who fulsome praise extends,
Shows more emotion than your genuine friends. 760
filings have been said with wine to probe. and ply
Those whose trustworthiness they'd wish to try.
If you will write, let not bland smiles and bows
A fond opinion of your verses rouse.

Quintilius, had he heard your verses read, If aught displeased him, would at once have said, " These lines you'll please correct." Had you replied, That to improve them you in vain had tried, " Then blot them out," he'd say, and order you To send your verses to be forged anew. 770

If you preferred your errors to defend,
Rather than strive your verses to amend,
80 *A Judicious Friend*
Nullum ultra verbum aut operam insumebat inanem,
Quin sine rivali teque et tua solus amares.

Vir bonus et prudens versus reprehendet inertes, 445
Culpabit duros, incomptis allinet atrum
Transverso calamo signum, ambitiosa recidet
Ornamenta, parum claris lucem dare coget,
Arguet ambigue dictum, mutanda notabit;
Fiet Aristarchus; nec dicet, " Cur ego amicum 450
Offendam in nugis ?" Hse nugse seria ducent
In mala derisum semel exceptumque sinistre.

Ut mala quem scabies aut morbus regius urget, Aut fanaticus error, et iracunda Diana,

not waste another word, or throw away his useless labour, but you might, *at far as he was concerned,* expend your fondness on yourself and your own compositions without a rival. A good and sensible man will censure spiritless verses, will find fault with what are harsh, will fix a black obliterating mark with an inverted pen upon what are inelegant, will cut away ornaments which hare an affectation of splendour, will compel you to throw light upon what are not sufficiently clear, will arraign what has been ambiguously said, will point out what ought to be altered. He will, in short, become an Aristarchus. Nor will he say, " Why should I give offence to my friend in the case of trifles *t"* These trifles will lead to serious evils, if lie has been once made a dupe of by satirical praise, and thus treated treacherously and unfairly.

Those who are wise fear to have

touched, and fly away from, a mad poet, as they would from a man whom an evil leprosy, or the expensive disease of jaundice, oppresses, or frantic madness or lunacy. Boys knock him about

makes a Faithful Critic. 81
He would not deign to add another word,
To waste his labour would have been absurd,
He'd leave you to yourself to spend your love
Upon the poems you'd so much approve.
A kind judicious man will always blame
Verses unworthy of their author's name,
Find fault with what are harsh, erase the bad,
Those that want spirit, and are coarsely made: 780
Ambitious splendours he will prune away,
Shed on what's dark a bright revealing ray,
What's said with doubtful meaning ho'll arraign,
What should bo changed, and what bo made more plain;
He will, in fact, an Aristarchus be,
Who could not bear the slightest fault to see;
Nor will he say, " Why should I fear to offend,
In what arc trifles, my respected friend ?"
These trifles lead to worse, if you conceal,
Unkind, uncandid, what you think and feel. 790
Just as we dread a man with jaundice ill,
Or one whom wild and frenzied fancies fill,

82 *Humorous Description* '
Vesanum tetigisse timerit fugiuntque poetam, 455
Qui sapiunt; agitant pueri, incautique sequuntur.
Hie, dum sublimis versus ructatur, et errat,
Si, veluti merulis intentus, decidit, auceps,
In puteum foveamve, 'licet, " Succurrite," longum
Clamet, " Io cives !" non sit qui tollere curet. - 460
Si curet quis opem ferre et demittere funcm,
" Qui scis an prudens hue se projecerit, atque
Servari nolit ?" dicam, Siculique poeto
Narrabo interitum. Deus immortalis haberi
Dum cupit Empedocles, ardentem frigidus jEtnam
Insiluit . Sit jus liceutquo perire poetis: 466

and incautiously follow him. If, while in a pompous aspiring attitude he is pouring forth his verses and is wandering at large, he falls into a well or a pit like a fowler intent upon his game, although he should cry out for a long time, " Help me, ye citizens !" let there not be one who would care to lift him out . If any one' should feel a concern to lend him assistance and to let down a rope – " How do you know whether he threw himself in here intentionally, and does not wish to be saved ?" I will say; and will relate the death of the Sicilian bard. While Empedocles desires to be considered a god, he leaped in a shivering fit into burning ./Etna. Let poets have the liberty and the privilege

of a Mad Poet, 83
Those who have sense a frantic poet fear
And dread to touch him or to feel him near.
Boys shove him here and there, unguarded chase,
Pursue him just for sport from place to place.
If, while with air erect he spouts his rhyme,'
Just like a fowler who expends his time
In seeking game, he falls into a snare,
Let not a passing townsman kindly care . 800
To lift him out, though he should loudly cry –
" Have pity, friends, and save me or I die."
If any one should wish to lend a hand,
" How do you know but his destruction's planned,
And that he schemed it in his own mad brain,
And does not wish to be restored again ?"
I say; and tell of the Sicilian bard
Who into burning Etna coldly dared
To leap, because he wished to have the fame
And *falat* of a god's immortal name. 810
Let poets choose the privilege to die
By any mode their fancy likes to try.
84 *And of his Importunate*
Invitum qui servat, idem facit occidenti.

Nee semel hoc fecit, nee si retractus erit, jam
Fiet homo, et ponet famosze mortis amorem.
Nee satis apparet cur versus factitet; utrum 470
Miuxerit in patrios cineres, an triste bideutal
Moverit incestus : certe furit, ac velut ursus, /
Objectos caveso valuit si frangere clathros,
Indoctum doctumquo fugat recitator acerbus;
Quem vero arripuit, tenet occiditque legendo, 475
Non missura cutem, nisi plena cruoris, hirudo.

to perish *at they like.* He who saves a man against his will docs the name as the man who kills him. Nor has ho done this only once, nor, if he shall bo recovered, will he now become a man and lay aside his lore for *the tdat of* a distinguished death. Nor does it sufficiently appear why he makes verses, whether he has polluted his father's ashes, or has impiously removed the melancholy trophy of devastations made by lightning. Undoubtedly he is raging mad, and, like the bear, if he has been able to break through the grates put up against his den, as a merciless reciter he persecutes both the unlearned and the learned alike. But whomever he has seized upon, he keeps and kills him by his reading, just like the leech which will not let go his hold of the skin unless it is full of blood.

THE END.

and Tormenting Annoyances. 85

He that would save a man against his will
Does just the same as if that man he'd kill.
Nor has he done this merely once, nor yet
If he's restored will he more wisdom get,
He will not be a man, nor lay aside
A wish to die to gratify his pride.
Nor why he writes no mortal tongue can say ;
Has he defiled his father's grave to-day ? 820
Or moved the sad memorial of the storm
Which marks where lightning flashed with dire alarm ?
No doubt he's mad, and, like the raging bear,
That bursts the barriers placed to guard his lair,
Unlearned and learned he persecutes the same,
Eecites his rhymes without remorse or shame ;
But whom he gets to listen to his verse,
He tortures and torments from worse to worse,
Annoys him, plagues him, takes away his breath,
And by his reading gives him up to death; 830
Just like a leech that sucks the purple gore,
And will not leave the skin till it can gorge no more.
THE KM).

rillXTCU UY WILLIAM BLACKWOOU AMI SONS.
3 2044 024 587 149
THE BORROWER WILL BE CHARGED

Lightning Source UK Ltd.
Milton Keynes UK
02 August 2010

157768UK00002B/194/P